FRENCH TRACTION

Andrew Cole

First published 2017

Amberley Publishing
The Hill, Stroud
Gloucestershire, GL5 4EP

www.amberley-books.com

Copyright © Andrew Cole, 2017

The right of Andrew Cole to be identified as the Author of this work has been asserted in accordance with the Copyrights, Designs and Patents Act 1988.

ISBN 978 1 4456 6617 4 (print)
ISBN 978 1 4456 6618 1 (ebook)

All rights reserved. No part of this book may be reprinted or reproduced or utilised in any form or by any electronic, mechanical or other means, now known or hereafter invented, including photocopying and recording, or in any information storage or retrieval system, without the permission in writing from the Publishers.

British Library Cataloguing in Publication Data.
A catalogue record for this book is available from the British Library.

Origination by Amberley Publishing.
Printed in the UK.

Introduction

Welcome to this collection of modern traction images from France. While not intended as a comprehensive guide to the railways of France, this book offers a compilation of photographic highlights from across the Channel. Due to its size, France has always been home to a large and varied selection of different classes of locomotives. The main operator in France is SNCF, *Société Nationale des Chemins de fer Français*, and the railways are still state owned.

Diesel locomotives can be seen working the length and breadth of the country, but electrically the country can be split in half. The northern part of the country runs off 25-kV AC overhead wires, whereas the southern half of the country runs off 1,500-V DC supply. There are approximately 20,000 miles of railway lines in France, with just over 1,000 of them high-speed lines.

Electric locomotives that only work in the south have running numbers containing four digits, whereas the electric locos in the north have five digits, starting with a '1'. The locos that run off both voltages have five digits that start with a '2', '3' or a '4'. The locos that start with a '3' also work under 3,000-V DC current.

All locomotives are now split between different operating sectors, ranging from passenger sectors to SNCF Fret and Infra.

A lot of French classes share the same body design, which includes some iconic body styling. The most numerous class of loco was the BB 63500 class. They shared the same body design as the BB 63000. Combined, there were nearly 1,000 of the type in use, although, like most of the older classes, most have since been withdrawn and scrapped. Some of the type have found use with VFLI, a subsidiary of SNCF.

Another large type of diesel loco was the BB 67000 class of locos. This class of loco, spread over different subclasses, totalled nearly 400; some are still in use today, with just a few clinging onto passenger workings. Some of the biggest diesels were the CC 72000 class of loco built by Alstom, which were used on both passenger and freight workings. Again, some are still in use today, although they've been re-engined.

There are also plenty of new Vossloh- and Alstom-built locos in use today in the BB 61000 and BB 75000 classes of locomotives. SNCF used to employ hundreds of small shunter locomotives but, with the general decline in traffic, most of these have been withdrawn; however, a rebuilding programme has meant that over 100 of the Y9000 type of shunter will be in use for many years.

On the electric locomotive front, there have again been many different types of loco used on both passenger and freight duties. Some of these classes share iconic body styling, the most notable being the *Nez Cassé* (broken nose) family of locomotives.

This body styling was shared between the CC 6500, BB 7200, BB 15000 and BB 22000 classes of locomotives. Again inroads are being made into these classes, with the CC 6500 being completely withdrawn.

During the 1960s, Alstom built a large family of mixed traffic locomotives, which also shared the same 'box' type of bodywork. These encompassed the BB 8500, BB 16500, BB 17000, BB 20200 and the BB 25500 locos.

There are many modern electric locos in use in France as well, ranging from BB 26000 'Sybic' locos to BB 27000 'Prima' locomotives.

All in all, despite mass withdrawal of older types of locomotives (indeed, there is a huge storage yard at Sotteville, Rouen, which houses many of these withdrawn locos), there is still plenty left on the railways of France to interest the locomotive enthusiast.

Akiem No. 37026, 22 July 2015

No. 37026 passes through Köln West in Germany with a light engine move. This loco carries SNCF Fret livery, but is operated by Akiem. Fifty of these electric locomotives were built by Alstom from 2002 onwards.

CBR No. 37519, 21 July 2015

CB Rail Prima locomotive No. 37519 is seen at Düsseldorf Rath station in Germany with a rake of open wagons. There are over thirty of these privately owned Alstom Prima locos in use, and they are in the number series 37/5.

ECR No. 77008, 9 February 2014

No. 77008 is seen stabled for the weekend at Caffiers Faisceau d'Exchanges. This loco is operated by ECR, Euro Cargo Rail, which is a subsidiary of DB Cargo. The Class 77 locomotive is identical to the British Class 66, apart from the addition of a roof-mounted air con system.

SNCF No. 0007, 22 June 2002

No. 0007 is seen resting at Nevers depot, Bourgogne, carrying a blue-and-white livery. The small diesel shunters that go into internal use at depots and works are known as 'Locmas', this one being Locma No. 0007. It was renumbered from Y2266.

SNCF No. 1102, 13 November 2001

No. 1102 stands condemned at Villeneuve St Georges depot, Paris. This was a class of twelve electric locomotives, and all have now been withdrawn. No. 1102 was built in 1938 and was withdrawn in 2000.

SNCF No. 6501, 18 August 2001

No. 6501 is seen at Villeneuve St Georges depot, Paris, carrying Grand Confort livery, which suited the class well. This class of locomotives was built to a design that was widely used in France, and is known as *Nez Cass*é, or 'broken nose'.

SNCF No. 6506, 11 November 2001

No. 6506 is seen at rest at Vénissieux depot, Lyon. By this time the locomotive had been repainted into SNCF Fret livery, and had lost its name, *Vierzon*.

SNCF No. 6523, 12 November 2001

No. 6523 *Brive* is seen stabled at St Jean de Maurienne depot, Savoie, carrying Grand Confort livery; meanwhile, a classmate behind carries SNCF Fret livery. There were a total of seventy-eight of these locomotives in use, but all have now been withdrawn from service.

SNCF No. 6560, 11 October 1997

No. 6560 is seen poking out of the very impressive roundhouse at Villeneuve St Georges depot, Paris. No. 6560 carries Grand Confort livery, while the name *Oullins* can be seen in the middle of the body in grey.

SNCF No. 7214, 12 July 2002

No. 7214 is seen in SNCF grey livery while stabled at Les Aubrais depot, Orléans. Notably, at this time the loco still retains its cast SNCF logo on the cab front.

SNCF No. 7221, 12 July 2002

No. 7221 is seen in Corail Plus livery at Bordeaux depot. This loco carries the name *Saint-Amand-Montrond*, while its livery was for passenger workings. A total of 220 of these locomotives were built from 1976 onwards; most are still in traffic, but a few are in storage.

SNCF No. 7232, 8 February 2014

No. 7232 leads a line of stored BB 7200 locomotives at Sotteville yard, Rouen. This is a large storage facility in the north of France that holds over 400 stored and condemned locomotives. No. 7232 used to be named *Souillac*.

SNCF No. 7248, 11 October 1997
No. 7248 is seen stabled at Sud Ouest depot, Paris, surrounded by many other electric locomotives. Note that the loco stands over the old steam pits, and that it still retains the cast SNCF on the cab front.

SNCF No. 7258, 19 August 2000
No. 7258 is seen resting in the roundhouse at Villeneuve St Georges depot, Paris. This is another passenger-liveried loco, carrying Corail Plus livery. The Class BB 7200 locos only run on 1500-V DC.

SNCF No. 7263, 30 June 2001

No. 7263 is seen working through Bourges station on a passenger working. Note this loco has had an addition to the running number – an extra '1' and '0'. This indicates that the loco belonged to the SNCF Voyages high-speed services sector.

SNCF No. 7279, 8 February 2014

No. 7279 is seen in long-term storage at Sotteville yard, Rouen. The number of withdrawn and stored locomotives at this location is staggering.

SNCF No. 7295, 25 June 2000

No. 7295 rests in the sun at Les Aubrais depot, Orléans. This is another Class BB 7200 locomotive that worked for the SNCF Voyages high-speed services sector at the time, the '1' and '0' before the running number being the giveaway. Note that the running number on the front is placed where the cast SNCF logo used to be.

SNCF No. 7300, 13 July 2002

No. 7300 is seen stabled at Bordeaux depot, carrying grey and orange livery, and is complete with the black-and-white SNCF on the front. The Class BB 7200 series are DC locos; the Class BB 15000 are AC locomotives; and the dual voltage is the BB 22000 locomotives, with 7200 and 15000 together equaling 22000. All locomotives share the same body design.

SNCF No. 7387, 25 June 2000

No. 7387 is seen at rest at Les Aubrais depot, Orléans. This loco carries a '4' and a '0' before the running number, indicating that this loco belonged to the SNCF Fret sector as a freight loco.

SNCF No. 7406, 19 August 2000

No. 7406 is seen on one of the roundhouse roads at Villeneuve St Georges depot, Paris. At this time, the loco still retained all its cast logos and numbers on the front and bodyside.

SNCF No. 7407, 17 August 2002

No. 7407 basks in the summer sunshine at Sud Ouest depot, Paris. Classmate No. 7314 can be seen to the right.

SNCF No. 7411, 11 October 1997

No. 7411 is seen preparing to take a ride on the turntable at Villeneuve St Georges depot, Paris. This loco carries the name *Lamure-sur-Azergues*. Fourteen members of this class were converted to BB 7600 for passenger work out of Paris Montparnasse.

SNCF No. 8120, 2 June 2001
No. 8120 is seen stabled at Dijon Perigny depot, alongside No. 36021. Nearly 200 of these locos were built by Alstom from 1948 onwards, and all have now been withdrawn.

SNCF No. 8123, 13 November 2001
No. 8123 rests outside the roundhouse at Villeneuve St Georges depot, Paris. Note that this loco has gained the numbers '4' and '0' before the running number, indicating its use by the freight sector SNCF Fret.

SNCF No. 8187, 11 November 2001
No. 8187 is seen stabled at Portes-lès-Valence depot, Valence. The loco has been stabled off the electrified sidings, and was not withdrawn until 2004.

SNCF No. 8212, 11 November 2001
No. 8212 is seen stabled on one of the roundhouse roads at Vénissieux depot, Lyon. This is another Class BB 8100 loco to be operated by the SNCF Fret sector.

SNCF No. 8257, 18 August 2001

No. 8257 is seen stabled at Sud Ouest depot, Paris, still carrying the old green livery. Like most of the later numbered Class BB 8100 locos, this would be withdrawn carrying this livery.

SNCF Nos 8271, 8266 and 8252, 17 August 2002

Nos 8271, 8266 and 8252 are all seen stabled at Sud Ouest depot, Paris. Of note is the fact that, at the time, the depot still used a traverser to stable some of the locomotives. At this time, there were five of these Class BB 8100 locos allocated to Sud Ouest for empty stock workings out of Paris Austerlitz station.

SNCF No. 8563, 11 October 1997

No. 8563 is seen stabled at Sud Ouest depot, Paris, still retaining its early green livery. This would be the last Class BB 8500 loco to carry this livery. Of note is the attractive SNCF badge on the loco front, which encompasses the running number in one big casting.

SNCF No. 8564, 11 October 1997

No. 8564 rests at Sud Ouest depot, Paris, carrying the standard SNCF grey-and-orange (beton) livery. This loco would be withdrawn in 2004 from Toulouse depot.

SNCF No. 8585, 31 March 2001

No. 8585 is seen in grey-and-orange livery at Trappes depot, Paris. From 1964 onwards, nearly 150 of these locos were built by Alstom to another body design that would be used on various classes.

SNCF No. 8587, 8 February 2014

No. 8587 is another locomotive in long-term storage at Sotteville yard, Rouen. There are just a very small handful of these locos still in use. No. 8587 has received the numbers '5' and 'o' before the running number, indicating it was last used by the Action Régionale (Regional Passenger) sector.

SNCF No. 8591, 25 June 2000

No. 8591 is seen stabled at Trappes depot, Paris. This loco carries Île-de-France livery, and was used on passenger work. The numbers '8' and '0' have been inserted before the running number to indicate that it is an Île-de-France loco.

SNCF No. 8595, 17 August 2002

No. 8595 is seen stabled at Montrouge depot, Paris, at the head of a passenger working, ready for the next day's workings. This loco carries Île-de-France livery for passenger workings out of Paris.

SNCF Nos 9201 and 9284, 13 July 2002

Nos 9201 and 9284 are seen stabled side by side at Bordeaux depot. No. 9201 carries SNCF Fret livery, whereas No. 9284 carries Corail Plus livery.

SNCF No. 9210, 11 October 1997

No. 9210 rests at Villeneuve St Georges depot, Paris, carrying green livery. Ninety-two of these locomotives were built by Jeumont-Schneider from 1957 onwards, and all are now withdrawn.

SNCF No. 9228, 4 December 1999

No. 9228 is seen stabled at Villeneuve St Georges depot, Paris, under a very threatening sky. This class of loco, like all other classes with four-digit numbers, only ran under 1500-V DC wires.

SNCF No. 9238, 12 July 2002

No. 9238 passes through Poitiers station at the head of a freight working, carrying the correct SNCF Fret livery for the duty. This loco has gained the numbers '4' and '0', indicating that it is an SNCF Fret loco.

SNCF No. 9256, 24 June 2002

No. 9256 is seen stabled at Tours station, carrying Multi Services livery. This livery suited this class well, but was only carried by six members.

SNCF No. 9269, 25 June 2002

No. 9269 is preparing to depart from Le Mans station with a passenger working while carrying standard grey-and-orange livery – this was known as Beton livery, which literally translates to concrete. This loco has been preserved at Amberieu.

SNCF No. 9282, 8 February 2014

No. 9282 is seen in long-term storage at Sotteville yard, Rouen. This loco carries En Voyage livery, and has gained the numbers '5' and '0' before the running number, indicating that it was last used by the Action Régionale (Regional Passenger) sector.

SNCF No. 9290, 12 July 2002

No. 9290 is seen carrying Multi Services livery at Les Aubrais depot, Orléans. This loco carries the numbers '1' and '0' before the running number, indicating it was in use with the SNCF Voyages high-speed sector.

No. SNCF 9326, 17 August 2002

No. 9326 is seen stabled at Villeneuve St Georges depot, Paris. This loco carries the name *Montrabe*, and was one of only two Class BB 9300 locos to receive names. Forty of this class of loco were built by Jeumont-Schneider from 1967 onwards. All have now been withdrawn, with two preserved.

SNCF No. 9604, 11 November 2001

No. 9604 is seen stabled at Vénissieux depot, Lyon, carrying grey-and-orange livery. The Class BB 9600 locos were converted from BB 9400 locos; the conversion included the fitting of multiple-working equipment on the loco front. No. 9604 was converted from No. 9426.

SNCF No. 9641, 24 June 2002

No. 9641 is seen at Tours station at the head of a passenger working. This loco carries a special livery for these workings, which it shared with No. 9642. No. 9641 carries the name *Tours*.

SNCF No. 9701, 19 August 2000

No. 9701 is seen stabled at Sud Ouest depot, Paris. This loco was converted from 9271, and was one of four such locos converted for Paris to Laroche-Migennes passenger workings.

SNCF No. 9703, 17 August 2002
No. 9703 spends the weekend stabled at Sud Ouest depot, Paris. This loco was converted from No. 9285 for passenger workings from Paris to Laroche-Migennes.

SNCF No. 12008, 7 October 1995
No. 12008 is seen condemned at Lens depot, near Calais, at the head of a long line of similarly condemned sister locomotives. 148 members of this class were built by various builders from 1955 onwards, and all have been withdrawn.

SNCF No. 12010, 20 January 2002.
No. 12010 is seen condemned at Lens depot, near Calais. By this time all the members of this class had been withdrawn. Like all other classes that have five digits starting with a '1', these locos only ran under 25-kV AC lines.

SNCF No. 12046, 5 June 2001
No. 12046 is another member of the class that stands condemned at Lens depot. At this time, Lens was full of condemned Class BB 12000 locomotives awaiting the cutter's torch.

SNCF No. 12100, 5 June 2001
No. 12100 contemplates its future at Lens depot as it stands condemned along with many other classmates.

SNCF No. 12106, 20 January 2002
No. 12106 is seen at Lens depot, having been condemned. A start has been made in stripping the loco for spare parts, including removing the nose section.

SNCF No. 12143, 22 June 1997

No. 12143 is seen resting outside the magnificent depot building at Châlons-sur-Marne, near Reims. At the time, this loco only had a further two years' service left, being withdrawn in 1999 – the year in which the last members of the class were withdrawn. This view shows the beautifully combined SNCF number panel.

SNCF No. 14131, 21 June 1997

No. 14131 is seen condemned at Thionville depot, north-east France, near Luxembourg. This loco belonged to a class of just over 100 locos, and was a Co-Co version of the BB 12000 class. All are withdrawn, and two have been preserved.

SNCF No. 15001, 18 August 2002
No. 15001 is seen in the servicing bay at La Villette depot, Paris. This loco carries Grand Confort livery as well as the name *Gretz-Armainvilliers*.

SNCF No. 15002, 7 October 2000
No. 15002 is seen waiting to depart from Luxembourg station with a passenger working to Paris. This loco carries Grand Confort livery as well as the name *Longwy*. The BB 15000 class is an AC version of the BB 7200 locomotives.

SNCF No. 15008, 19 August 2001
No. 15008 is seen in Grand Confort livery at La Villette depot, Paris. This loco carries the name *Nancy*, which can be seen on the bodyside in the middle of the loco.

SNCF No. 15016, 21 June 1997
No. 15016 *Charleville-Mezieres* is seen at Luxembourg, waiting to depart for Paris. This loco carries Corail Plus livery.

SNCF No. 15027, 21 June 1997
No. 15027 spends the weekend stabled at Thionville depot, north-east France. This loco carries Corail Plus livery and the name *Creutzwald*.

SNCF No. 15037, 8 February 2014
No. 15037 is seen stabled at Le Havre station. This loco carries the name *La Ferte-Sous-Jouarre*, and has had a number 1 added to the front of its running number, denoting its operation by the SNCF Voyages high-speed sector.

SNCF Nos 15042 and 15043, 19 August 2001

No. 15042 *Etival-Clairfontaine* is seen side by side with classmate No. 15043, *Maizieres Les Metz*, at La Villette depot, Paris. Both locos carry Corail Plus livery; notably No. 15042 has received a number 1 in front of its running number, whereas No. 15043 has yet to receive a number.

SNCF No. 15045, 5 December 1999

No. 15045 is seen stabled at La Villette depot, Paris, carrying Grand Confort livery. This loco also carries the name *Raon L'etape*.

SNCF No. 15046, 8 February 2014
No. 15046 is seen stabled at Le Havre station, carrying Corail Plus livery. This loco doesn't carry a name and has had the number 5 added to its running number, meaning that it is operated by the Action Régionale (Regional Passenger) sector. It also has the letter 'R' added, just to make sure.

SNCF No. 16003, 8 February 2014
No. 16003 rests in the big storage yard at Sotteville while carrying En Voyage passenger livery. Sixty-two of these AC electric locos were built from 1958 onwards by MTE, Le Matériel de Traction Électrique.

SNCF No. 16008, 8 February 2014

No. 16008 is another loco in long-term storage at Sotteville yard, Rouen. This loco carries En Voyage livery; the black panel at the far end of the loco is where the image of a woman's and a child's faces used to be, but they have been painted out on all the En Voyage-liveried locos in the yard.

SNCF No. 16018, 13 March 1999

No. 16018 is seen waiting to depart from Le Havre, north-west France, with a passenger working. This loco was withdrawn in 2009, still carrying this livery.

SNCF No. 16024, 13 March 1999

No. 16024 runs into Sotteville station with a passenger working while still carrying Beton livery. This view shows how low some of the platforms are on the Continent, and the need for steps on the carriages.

SNCF No. 16043, 8 February 2014

No. 16043 sits forlornly at Sotteville yard, along with many other stored locomotives. This loco carries Multi Services livery, and was withdrawn at the end of 2012. Fifteen members of the BB 16000 class would be rebuilt, becoming the BB 16100 class.

SNCF No. 16108, 8 February 2014
No. 16108 is seen at the locomotive storage facility at Sotteville yard, Rouen. This loco was built in the late 1950s by MTE as No. 16026, and was rebuilt in the early 1990s to become No. 16108. The conversion allowed the members of this class to work in push-pull mode.

SNCF No. 16114, 8 February 2014
No. 16114 leads a long line of other stored electric locomotives at Sotteville yard, Rouen. This loco was converted from No. 16062, and the fifteen locomotives were converted to work in push-pull mode on the Paris Nord–Saint-Quentin and Amiens route. They also appeared on the Paris St Lazare–Rouen line. All fifteen members have been withdrawn.

SNCF No. 16511, 7 October 1995

No. 16511 is seen stabled at Lille Flanders station at the head of a rake of push-pull single-deck carriages. Nearly 300 of these AC-powered locomotives were built from 1958 onwards by Alstom, and they share the same body design as the BB 8500, BB 17000, BB 20200 and BB 25500 classes of locomotives.

SNCF No. 16525, 7 October 1995

No. 16525 is seen at Lens station, north-west France, with a rake of double-deck push-pull carriages. This was my very first visit to France, and I remember thinking how very different the SNCF locomotives looked when compared to the British locomotives.

SNCF No. 16528, 19 January 2003
No. 16528 rests between duties at Somain depot, north-east France. This depot is situated not far from the Belgian border. No. 16528 carries Beton livery, which was adopted by most members of this class.

SNCF No. 16531, 5 June 2001
No. 16531 is seen at Lens station with a rake of single-deck push-pull carriages while carrying Beton livery. All members of this class were withdrawn by 2011.

SNCF No. 16556, 12 October 1997
No. 16556 leads a line up of five BB 16500 locos at La Villette depot, Paris. This was a large depot that serviced electric locomotives for use out of Gare du Nord station.

SNCF No. 16557, 5 June 2001
No. 16557 is seen stabled at Lens depot while still carrying green livery. This loco was one of just four members of this class that stayed in green livery until withdrawal, with No. 16557 withdrawn in 2002. No. 16557 stands on accommodation bogies while its own are under repair.

SNCF No. 16564, 17 August 2002
No. 16564 is seen stabled at Acheres depot, Paris. This was another member of this class of loco that carried green livery until withdrawal, with No. 16564 leaving service just four months later.

SNCF No. 16581, 18 August 2002
No. 16581 basks in the summer sunshine at La Villette depot, Paris, while carrying Beton livery. This loco would be withdrawn less than twelve months later, but the final members of the class would survive until 2011.

SNCF No. 16583, 24 March 2001

No. 16583 is seen stabled at La Gare de l'Est station in Paris. This loco carries Île-de-France passenger livery, and also has the correct extra digit in front of the running number. This was the only member of the class to be withdrawn carrying this livery.

SNCF No. 16614, 8 February 2014

No. 16614 is seen withdrawn in the yard at Sotteville, Rouen. This loco had been withdrawn four years earlier, but still looks to be in reasonable condition.

SNCF No. 16635, 27 April 1996
No. 16635 is seen at La Gare de l'Est station, Paris, while still carrying green livery. This is another class of loco that had the impressive cast number and SNCF logo on the front.

SNCF No. 16648, 25 June 2002
No. 16648 is seen stabled at Achères depot, Paris, while carrying SNCF Fret livery. Just six members of the class received this livery. This loco also has the number 4 before its running number to indicate that it is operated by SNCF Fret.

SNCF No. 16690, 4 June 2001

No. 16690 is seen stabled at Thionville depot. This depot is in the north-east of France, not far from the big yards at Woippy and Metz. Of note at this depot is the lack of overhead wires, with the locos shunted into the sidings by diesel.

SNCF No. 16772, 19 January 2002

No. 16772 is seen at Compiegne station with a rake of single-deck carriages. This station is situated north-east of Paris, and No. 16772 has not long been overhauled, including a repaint into Beton livery.

SNCF No. 16779, 19 August 2001

No. 16779 rests at La Villette depot, Paris, carrying SNCF Fret livery. Only six members of the BB 16500 class received this livery.

SNCF No. 17001, 18 August 2001

No. 17001 is seen carrying Île-de-France passenger livery at Achères depot, Paris. 105 of these locomotives were built by Alstom from 1965 onwards and they were built for suburban passenger workings out of Paris. Their numbers have been thinned recently with a lot of their workings being taken over by modern EMUs.

SNCF No. 17015, 8 February 2014

No. 17015 is seen withdrawn at Sotteville yard, Rouen, carrying Île-de-France passenger livery. This loco had been withdrawn six years earlier, and today there are just over thirty left in use.

SNCF No. 17017, 11 October 1997

No. 17017 is seen stabled at Achères depot, Paris, while still carrying Beton livery. Most members of this class went on to receive Île-de-France passenger livery.

SNCF No. 17063, 8 February 2014
No. 17063 stands condemned at Sotteville yard, Rouen, with a start already being made to strip the loco for spare parts. No. 17063 still carries Île-de-France passenger livery, and was withdrawn from La Chapelle depot, Paris, in 2009.

SNCF No. 20212, 3 June 2001
No. 20212 is seen stabled at Hausbergen yard carrying Beton livery. Just thirteen members of this class were built in 1970, and they were capable of operating off 1500-V DC as well as 25-kV AC electric systems. They were used mainly in the Strasburg area; all are now withdrawn, with one preserved at the SNCF museum, Mulhouse.

SNCF No. 22204, 8 February 2014
No. 22204 is seen in long-term storage at Sotteville yard, Rouen. The BB 22200 class are dual-voltage locomotives, able to run off 1500-V DC as well as 25-kV AC power supplies. 205 of these locos were built by Alstom from 1976 onwards, and most are still in service today, although there are a few in store at Sotteville.

SNCF No. 22232, 24 June 2002
No. 22232 stands in the early morning sunshine at Tours depot, carrying Beton livery. The loco is seen coupled to a rake of single-deck carriages.

SNCF No. 22267, 8 February 2014

No. 22267 stands condemned at Sotteville yard, Rouen. This loco looks in very poor condition, with all of the side grills and one of the pantographs missing, while the Beton paintwork is looking very faded. This loco once carried the name *La Ciotat*.

SNCF No. 22298, 12 July 2002

No. 22298 is seen stabled at Poitiers depot, carrying Beton livery. The loco has received the number 4 in front of the running number, indicating that it is operated by the SNCF Fret sector.

SNCF No. 22299, 9 February 2014
No. 22299 is seen stabled at Sotteville depot, Rouen. Despite not carrying an extra digit, this loco is operated by the Infrastructure sector and so should have a number 6 in front of the running number.

SNCF No. 22317, 25 August 1992
No. 22317 *La-Tour-Du-Pin* is seen on the back of a low loader on Chester Road, Birmingham. This loco had been sent over for the Freight connection exhibition at the NEC in Birmingham, and was on its way to be displayed. This was the very first foreign loco that I saw.

SNCF No. 22323, 14 March 1999

No. 22323 *Cagnes-Sur-Mer* is seen stabled at Rennes depot. This loco still carries Beton grey-and-orange livery, which most members of the class carried.

SNCF No. 22365, 8 February 2014

No. 22365 stands at Sotteville yard, Rouen, while in long-term storage. The loco carries SNCF Fret livery, and also has the correct digit, '4', before the running number. This is one of just a small handful of these locos to carry this livery.

SNCF No. 22399, 19 August 2000

No. 22399 *Mormant* is seen poking out of the roundhouse at Villeneuve St Georges depot, Paris. This was one of nine Class BB 22200 locos that were hired to Railfreight Distribution for hauling freight trains through the Channel Tunnel in 1994 until enough British Class 92 locomotives were available for traffic.

SNCF No. 25108, 23 June 2000

No. 25108 is seen stabled at Châlons-sur-Marne depot carrying Beton livery. Twenty-five of these dual-voltage locos were built by MTE from 1964 onwards, and all are now withdrawn from service. Three were later sold to GFR in Romania.

SNCF No. 25237, 19 January 2003
No. 25237 is seen at Beauvais with a passenger working. The loco carries Multi Services livery, and is one of a class of fifty-one locos built by MTE from 1965 onwards. All are now withdrawn, but fourteen have been sold to GFR and exported to Romania.

SNCF No. 25523, 18 August 2001
No. 25523 is seen on the turntable at Villeneuve St Georges depot, Paris, while carrying SNCF Fret livery. This particular loco was withdrawn from service in 2006, and was sold to Regiotrans in Romania.

SNCF No. 25532, 01 April 2001

No. 25532 is seen carrying Multi Services livery at Vaires depot, Paris. Just under 200 of these dual-voltage locos were built by Alstom from 1964 onwards and are very similar to the Class BB 8500 and BB 17000 locos; if you add the numbers together, they equal the BB 25500.

SNCF No. 25569, 19 August 2001

No. 25569 is seen stabled at Vaires depot, Paris, carrying Multi Services livery. There are a few of these locos still in use as mixed-traffic locos.

SNCF No. 25590, 11 October 1997
No. 25590 is seen carrying Beton livery while stabled at Achères depot, Paris. This is one of a handful of this class of loco still in use today.

SNCF No. 26011, 17 August 2002
No. 26011 passes through Villeneuve Triage, carrying the standard livery for this class. Over 230 of these locos were built by GEC Alstom from 1988 onwards, and a start has been made in withdrawing these locos. No. 26011 carries the name *Le Piennois*.

SNCF Nos 26030 and 26025, 4 December 1999

Nos 26030 and 26025 are seen side by side at Villeneuve St Georges depot, Paris. This class of locos are known as 'Sybics', and are used as a mixed-traffic loco.

SNCF No. 26049, 4 June 2001

No. 26049 stands at Thionville depot, waiting its next turn of duty. This class of loco is used all over the country on both passenger and freight workings.

SNCF No. 26070, 5 June 2001

No. 26070 is seen stabled at Lens depot, north-west France, carrying a special Alsace Region livery. Despite the modern appearance, a start has been made in withdrawing this class of loco, with nearly thirty being taken out of traffic.

SNCF No. 26086, 8 October 2000

No. 26086 is seen carrying SNCF Fret livery at Châlons-sur-Marne depot. This is one of the 'Sybic' locos that have been withdrawn from traffic.

SNCF No. 26099, 7 October 1995
No. 26099 is seen stabled at Lens depot, north-west France. No. 26099 carries the standard livery that this class of locos carried.

SNCF No. 26099, 8 February 2014
No. 26099 is seen in storage at Sotteville yard, Rouen. At this time there were three of these locos present; later on, all three were withdrawn, which is surprising for a relatively modern class of loco.

SNCF No. 26100, 5 June 2001

No. 26100 *Pompey* is seen stabled at Lens depot, north-west France. These are dual-voltage locos, which are used on both passenger and freight workings.

SNCF No. 26160, 8 August 1999

No. 26160 is seen carrying Multi Services livery at Conflans-sur-Marne depot. At this time there were three 'Sybic' locos in this livery; however, one has since been repainted, leaving just this loco and No. 26227 carrying these colours.

SNCF No. 26172, 8 February 2014

No. 26172 is seen in long-term storage at Sotteville yard, Rouen. This was later withdrawn, and has since been preserved at the SNCF railway museum, Mulhouse.

SNCF No. 26200, 17 August 2002

Nos 26200 and 26020 are seen side by side at Vaires depot. This view shows the extra headlight fitted to the 'Sybic' class from No. 26188 onwards. No. 26020 carries the name *Menton*.

SNCF No. 26221, 4 June 2001
No. 26221 is seen stabled at Forbach yard, waiting its next turn of duty. This has since been named *Montauban*. The loco carries the number 4 before the running number, indicating that it is operated by the SNCF Fret sector.

SNCF No. 27008, 10 November 2001
No. 27008 is seen stabled at Dijon Perigny depot, carrying SNCF Fret livery. 180 of these Alstom-built locos were produced from 2001 onwards, and all are in traffic today, with the exception of No. 27115, which was withdrawn due to collision damage. The class are split between SNCF and Akiem.

SNCF No. 36002, 13 November 2001

No. 36002 is seen on one of the roundhouse roads at Villeneuve St Georges depot, Paris. Sixty of these locos were built by Alstom from 1996 onwards, and are known as 'Astride' locos. They are tri-voltage locos, and are mainly used on freight workings.

SNCF No. 36021, 5 June 2001

No. 36021 rests between duties at Lens depot, north-west France. The first thirty of these locos carry red livery, while the last thirty members carry green livery.

SNCF No. 36036, 2 June 2001
No. 36036 stands at Dijon Perigny depot, carrying green livery. This was later renumbered as 36336.

SNCF No. 36331, 8 October 2014
No. 36331 *Bons En Chablais/Castione Della Presolana* passes through Milano Certosa with a short steel working. This was originally delivered as No. 36031, and also carries the 'E' prefix for use in Italy.

SNCF FRET 1, 8 February 2014

FRET 1 is seen condemned at Sotteville yard, Rouen. This loco was built in 1957 by De Dietrich as Y6588. The loco would eventually become part of the Locma fleet of shunting locos, and was repainted green and numbered FRET 1, and also carried the number AT2 RO 203.

SNCF No. 60010, 9 February 2014

No. 60010 rests at Sotteville depot, Rouen, while it undergoes repairs. 175 of these locos were delivered from Vossloh from 2006 onwards.

SNCF No. 60027, 8 February 2014
No. 60027 is seen stabled at Sotteville depot, Rouen, carrying the attractive SNCF Fret green livery. It also displays the correct '4' before the running number.

SNCF No. 60121, 9 February 2014
No. 60121 is seen at Sotteville depot, Rouen, carrying SNCF Fret livery. 160 of these locomotives are operated by the Fret sector, while the last fifteen are operated by the Infra sector.

SNCF No. 60169, 8 February 2014
No. 60169 is seen carrying Infra yellow livery at Sotteville depot, Rouen. Note how this loco carries a number 6 before the running number, denoting that it is operated by the Infra sector. Sister locos can be seen in the background, carrying SNCF Fret livery.

SNCF No. 62001, 7 October 1995
No. 62001 is seen condemned at Lens depot, north-west France. This class of locomotives numbered 100 members, and they were built by the Baldwin Locomotive Works. They rode on A-1-A A-1-A bogies, and all have been withdrawn, but a few have been preserved.

SNCF No. 63007, 11 October 1997

No. 63007 rests at Sud Ouest depot, Paris, carrying green livery. The initial batch of this type of locomotive numbered 250 members, and they were built from 1953 onwards by Brissonneau and Lotz. This batch of locos has been withdrawn, with a few preserved.

SNCF No. 63032, 30 June 2001

No. 63032 is seen at Nevers depot, Bourgogne, while in the process of being scrapped. The orange livery this loco carried is known as 'Arzens'.

SNCF No. 63065, 24 June 2000
No. 63065 leads a line of six condemned BB 63000 locomotives at Nevers depot, Bourgogne. Of note is the fact that the cast numbers have been removed, but the cast SNCF on the loco front still remains.

SNCF No. 63066, 12 November 2001
No. 63066 is seen at Ambérieu depot, near Lyon, in the company of classmates Nos 63050 and 63042. All three locomotives had been withdrawn for four years, and all three had lost their cast SNCF logos from the front of the locos.

SNCF No. 63192, 8 February 2014
No. 63192 is seen in long-term storage at Sotteville yard, Rouen. This loco had been withdrawn ten years earlier, and a return to traffic is highly unlikely.

SNCF No. 63227, 29 June 2001
No. 63227 is seen carrying Arzens livery while on station pilot duty at Dijon station. This loco would last in service until 2005.

SNCF No. 63413, 6 September 1997

No. 63413 is seen stabled at Lens depot, carrying green livery. This loco would have a bright future, being preserved at the SNCF museum, Mulhouse. There were just twenty-three of the BB 63400 locos built by Brissonneau and Lotz, and are virtually identical to the large BB 63500 class of loco.

SNCF No. 63802, 25 June 2002

No. 63802 basks in the sunshine outside Trappes depot, just outside Paris. This large class of locomotives totalled nearly 600, and was used on both freight and passenger workings. Most have now been withdrawn, but some are still in service, including No. 63802, which now works for the Infra sector and still retains its green livery.

SNCF Nos 63819 and 63820, 8 August 1999
Consecutively numbered Nos 63819 and 63820 are seen side by side at Conflans-Jarny stabling point, and both carry Arzens livery. Both of these locomotives have now been withdrawn.

SNCF No. 64029, 8 February 2014
No. 64029 stands condemned at Sotteville yard, Rouen. This loco carries Arzens orange livery, but it has faded to a pink colour. This loco was last used by the Infra sector.

SNCF Nos 64816 and 64716, 19 January 2003

Master and slave locos Nos 64816 and 64716 are seen stabled at Lens depot, north-west France. These locos were rebuilt for heavy shunting duties, with No. 64816 being rebuilt from No. 63025, where the engine and all internals have been removed; the body was also lowered and shortened. The slave units only contain traction motors. No. 64716 was rebuilt from No. 63963, with little difference.

SNCF No. 66027, 8 February 2014

No. 66027 sits in Sotteville yard, Rouen, while in long-term storage. A start has been made on stripping the loco for spares, which includes the removal of the engine-room doors. Just over 300 of these loco were built by various companies from 1960 onwards.

SNCF No. 66078, 8 February 2014
No. 66078 leads a long line of withdrawn classmates in Sotteville yard, Rouen. Today there are less than thirty of these locos left in use, most working for the Infra sector. The ones at Sotteville are held in case traffic levels pick up, and are also a source of spares.

SNCF No. 66099, 20 January 2002
No. 66099 rests at La Deliverance yard, Lille, awaiting its next turn of duty. The blue-and-white livery sat well on this class of locomotives. Quite a few of this class of loco have been rebuilt as BB 69000 class locos.

SNCF No. 66153, 14 July 2002

No. 66153 is seen stabled at Sotteville depot, Rouen, carrying recently applied SNCF Fret livery. This was one of just ten members of the BB 66000 class of loco to receive this livery, and all ten have been withdrawn.

SNCF No. 66294, 14 July 2002

No. 66294 is seen basking in the summer sunshine at Sotteville depot, Rouen. Most members of this class were withdrawn, still carrying the blue-and-white livery, including No. 66294, which was withdrawn in 2011 from the Tours-St-Pierre depot.

SNCF No. 66607, 30 June 2001
No. 66607 is seen parked on the scrap lines at Nevers depot, Bourgogne. The BB 66600 class only numbered fewer than twenty examples, and some were rebuilt from BB 66000 locos. All were withdrawn by 1997.

SNCF No. 66717, 8 February 2014
No. 66717 is seen as part of a general view of the entrance to Sotteville yard, Rouen. This location houses over 400 stored and withdrawn locos, either awaiting stripping for spare parts or a return to service. The locos do change regularly, with some only staying in the yard for a short time. There are also now TGV power cars present, awaiting their fate.

SNCF No. 66717, 8 February 2014
No. 66717 rests at Sotteville yard, Rouen, while in long-term storage. This loco carries SNCF Fret livery. The BB 66700 class of loco were rebuilt from standard Class BB 66000 locos from 1985 onwards, with No. 66717 being rebuilt from No. 66149. Most have now been withdrawn, with just a very small handful working out of Thionville depot.

SNCF No. 67204, 11 October 1997
No. 67204 is seen stabled at Villeneuve St Georges depot, Paris. This was another standard design of locos that was spread over different classes and subclasses. The BB 67200 locos were rebuilt from the original BB 67000 class of loco, with No. 67204 being rebuilt from No. 67034.

SNCF No. 67210, 17 August 2002
No. 67210 is seen stabled at Creil Petite Therain yard, carrying Infra livery. This class of loco was rebuilt for working on the high-speed lines, and also for rescuing high-speed failures. This loco was rebuilt from No. 67120.

SNCF No. 67256, 13 November 2001
No. 67256 spends the weekend stabled at Villeneuve St Georges depot, Paris. Some members of this class were fitted with Scharfenberg couplings to rescue failed TGVs on the high-speed line. No. 67256 was rebuilt from No. 67085.

SNCF No. 67308, 8 February 2014

No. 67308 stands partially stripped at Sotteville yard, Rouen. There were originally seventy BB 67300 locos delivered, and a further twenty were rebuilt from BB 67000 locos. They were built by Brissonneau and Lotz from 1967 onwards as a mixed-traffic loco but, again, most of the class have been withdrawn from service.

SNCF No. 67476, 8 February 2014

No. 67476 stands in long-term storage at Sotteville yard, Rouen. The BB 67400 class of loco numbered just over 230 locomotives, and many are still in use today, both on freight and passenger workings. No. 67476 carries SNCF Fret livery, but this class of loco has carried many different liveries over the years.

SNCF No. 67533, 9 February 2014

No. 67533 is seen on a passenger working at Boulogne Ville station. This loco carries a '2' before the running number, indicating that it was operated by the Train Inter Regionaux (TIR) sector at the time. Their use on passenger workings is slowly coming to an end, with SNCF introducing large numbers of new units to replace them.

SNCF No. 68015, 24 June 2002

No. 68015 is seen stabled at Poitiers depot, West France. Eighty-one members of this class were built from 1963 onwards by various builders, and they were built to an A-1-A A-1-A wheel arrangement. A further four Class 68500 locos were re-engined and converted to Class 68000 locos. All have been withdrawn, except for No. 68081; some were rebuilt as Class 68500 locos.

SNCF No. 68083, 31 March 2001

No. 68083 is seen stabled at Trappes depot, just outside Paris. At this time the loco still carried all of its cast numbers and logos on the front and on the bodyside. This loco was originally built as No. 68525, but it was fitted with a Sulzer power unit, and was renumbered into the 68000 series.

SNCF No. 68538, 8 February 2014

No. 68538 stands at Sotteville yard, Rouen, among other locomotives stored long-term. This loco was the original member of this class, numbered 68501, but it was later fitted with a Sulzer engine and it was renumbered 68005. It later regained an AGO engine and was renumbered back into the 68500 series, becoming No. 68538. No. 68538 carries SNCF Fret livery, but has Infra markings. The '6' before the running number also indicates that it is an Infra loco.

SNCF No. 69228, 8 February 2014

No. 69228 is seen in storage at Sotteville yard, Rouen. At the time this loco was only in temporary storage, as this class of loco had only recently been rebuilt from BB 66000 locos, with No. 69228 being rebuilt from No. 66228.

SNCF Nos 72003 and 72015, 19 August 2001

Nos 72003 and 72015 are seen stabled side by side at La Plaine depot, Paris. There were ninety-two of these powerful locos built by Alstom from 1967 onwards. All were delivered as CC 72000 locos, but some have since been rebuilt with new engines and renumbered into the CC 72100 series. Today there are only three of the original locos left in use, and No. 72003 has since been sold to Morocco. No. 72015 carries the name *Paray-Le-Monial*.

SNCF No. 72007, 27 April 1996

No. 72007 is seen at La Gare Du Nord, Paris, with a passenger working. This loco would be withdrawn from Nevers depot in 2004.

SNCF No. 72020, 18 August 2002

No. 72020 is seen stabled at La Plaine depot, carrying SNCF Fret livery. Towards the end of their careers, most of the CC 72000 locos were used by SNCF Fret, with the passenger locos being re-engined and renumbered into the CC 72100 series.

SNCF No. 72025, 24 June 2002
No. 72025 is seen running light engine at Tours St Pierre station. This loco carries the name *Tarare*, which can be seen halfway along the bodyside. No. 72025 was withdrawn in 2005, still carrying blue livery, and is among many of the class stored at Sotteville yard, Rouen.

SNCF No. 72040, 1 April 2001
No. 72040 rests at La Plaine depot, Paris. This loco carries Corail Plus livery for use on passenger workings. This loco was renumbered as 72140 when it was fitted with a new SEMT Pielstick engine.

SNCF No. 72143, 8 February 2014

No. 72143 is seen condemned at Sotteville yard, Rouen. The loco carries En Voyage livery for passenger workings, and shows signs of the fire damage that resulted in its condemnation. On this day, there was another fire-damaged Class CC 72100 in the yard, with No. 72137 also being condemned. No. 72143 once carried the name *Langres*.

SNCF No. 75001, 9 February 2014

No. 75001 is seen stabled at Sotteville depot, Rouen. This is a member of a class of loco built by Alstom from 2006 onwards, and there were meant to be 400 members, although only 200 are in service. They are split between three different subclasses, with the BB 75000 being the standard loco.

SNCF No. 75089, 9 February 2014

No. 75089 is seen stabled at Sotteville depot, Rouen, carrying Infra livery, and also the correct '6' before the running number. This class is operated by both SNCF and Akiem, with the latter's locos leased to various operators and repainted into many different liveries. Some members of the class are being modified to work passenger services, and are renumbered into the BB 75300 series.

SNCF No. 75466, 9 February 2014

No. 75466 is seen carrying SNCF Fret livery at Sotteville depot, Rouen. The BB 75400 series locos are all operated by the SNCF Fret sector, and differ from the other subclasses by having a more environmentally friendly MTU engine.

SNCF No. 80002, 11 October 1997

No. 80002 is seen stabled at Sud Ouest depot, Paris. There were twelve members of this class of loco, and they were used for empty coaching stock moves at the terminal station in the Paris area. The class was rebuilt from BB 8100 locos, with No. 80002 being rebuilt from BB 8161.

SNCF Nos 80003 and 8266, 19 August 2000

Nos 80003 and 8266 are seen resting side by side at Sud Ouest depot, Paris. Both these locos were originally from the same class, but No. 80003 was rebuilt for empty coaching stock workings in the Paris area. As can be seen as part of the rebuild, No. 80003 has lost its multiple-working equipment from the front of the loco. No. 80003 was rebuilt from BB 8126.

SNCF No. 80010, 31 March 2001

No. 80010 is seen stabled on the traverser sidings at Sud Ouest depot, Paris, along with other members of the class. All locos in this view were used on empty coaching stock duties in the Paris area. No. 80010 was rebuilt from BB 8188, and was the last member of the class to be withdrawn, being condemned in 2010. It was later saved for preservation at Mohon. The other locos are Nos 80005, 8257, 80012, 8266 and 80003.

SNCF No. 88501, 8 February 2014

No. 88501 is seen condemned at Sotteville yard, Rouen. Thirty-one members of the BB 8500 class were converted to haul empty coaching stock in and out of the Paris terminal stations from 1997 onwards, being renumbered into the BB 88500 class in the process. All have now been withdrawn, their place being taken by Class BB 7200 locos.

SNCF No. 88511, 8 February 2014

No. 88511 sits condemned at Sotteville yard, Rouen. This loco was renumbered from BB 8511 when it was modified for hauling empty coaching stock trains in the Paris area. Out of the thirty-one members of this class, eight were further rebuilt as BB 8700 locos. No. 88511 has been earmarked for preservation at Mulhouse.

SNCF No. 88516, 11 October 1997

No. 88516 is seen stabled on one of the turntable roads at Villeneuve St Georges depot, Paris. This was renumbered from 8516 when it was modified for empty coaching stock duties in the Paris area. This was later renumbered to 8716.

SNCF No. 88529, 17 August 2002

No. 88529 is seen stabled at Sud Ouest depot, Paris. This was renumbered from 8529, and would be withdrawn in 2013.

SNCF Y5123, 12 July 2002

Y5123 is seen stabled at Bordeaux depot, carrying an attractive grey-and-red livery. This loco was built by De Dietrich in 1961 and was another shunter taken into the Locma fleet, being numbered 0069 and given the name *Pilou*. It has since been scrapped.

SNCF Y6577, 25 June 2000

Y6577 sits outside Les Aubrais depot, Orléans. This loco was built by De Dietrich in 1957 and was withdrawn in 1990; it has since been scrapped. There were over 200 of this Y6400 class of shunter built, split between builders De Dietrich and Decauville.

SNCF Y6623, 5 June 2001

Y6623 is seen stabled at Lens depot, north-west France, having just been repainted in green livery. This loco was built in 1958 by De Dietrich, and would be another shunter added to the Locma fleet. It was based at Somain Yard, not far from the Belgian border. Y6623 never received a Locma number, and has since been scrapped.

SNCF Y7129, 8 February 2014

Y7129 is seen in long-term storage at Sotteville Yard, Rouen. This class of locos numbered 210 members, and was built by Billard and Decauville from 1958 onwards. All have since been withdrawn. A large number of the class have been rebuilt as Class Y9000 shunters at Quatre Mares Works, Sotteville, including Y7129, which emerged as Y9088.

SNCF Y7458, 20 August 2000

Y7458 rests at La Plaine depot, Paris, waiting its next turn of duty. This was SNCF's largest class of shunter, with nearly 500 built from 1963 onwards, but all have been withdrawn. A large number of the class transferred to the Locma fleet, while others have been rebuilt into Y9000 shunters. Y7458 entered the Locma fleet, and is based at St Ouen, North Paris.

SNCF Y7568, 30 June 2001

Y7568 is seen stabled at Tours St Pierre depot, Tours. Y7568 was built by De Dietrich in 1966, and is currently stored.

SNCF Y7822, 14 March 1999

Y7822 is seen at Rennes depot, north-west France, while under going repairs with all of its engine-room doors removed. This loco was built by Moyse in 1971, and is seen carrying Arzens livery. This loco is currently stored, having not entered the Locma fleet, nor being rebuilt.

SNCF Y8203, 9 February 2014

Y8203 is seen stabled at Sotteville depot, Rouen. This class of locos numbered nearly 400 members, and was built by both Moyse and Fauvet Girel. Y8203 was built by Fauvet Girel in 1983 and, despite carrying SNCF Fret livery, it is operated by the Infra sector. Most of this class of shunter are still in use today. A further 150 locos were built from 1989 onwards, numbered in the Y8400 series.

SNCF Y8338, 9 February 2014

Y8338 is seen at Sotteville depot, Rouen. This loco was built in 1988 by Fauvet Girel, and is seen carrying Akiem grey livery. Of note is that a lot of these shunters have lost the 'Y' from their running number. A lot of the Akiem-allocated shunters are leased to other operators.

SNCF Y8372, 8 February 2014

Y8372 is seen in storage at Sotteville yard, Rouen. This loco would be removed from the storage lines and repainted into Akiem grey livery, but with SNCF Fret logos applied. Y8372 was built by Fauvet Girel in 1989.

SNCF Y9062, 9 February 2014

Y9062 is seen stabled at Sotteville depot, Rouen. This class of shunter has been rebuilt and re-engined from Y7100 and Y7400 locos, with eighty-eight rebuilt at Quatre Mares works, Rouen, and the first twenty-two members rebuilt at Tours. At present there are 110 of these rebuilt locos in use, and all carry the attractive Infra livery, which certainly makes them stand out. Y9062 was rebuilt from Y7408, and the locos are equipped with a new MAN engine.

SNCF Y9072, 8 February 2014

Y9072 is seen stabled in the storage yard at Sotteville, Rouen. This yard not only housed condemned locos but also locos waiting onward movement from the nearby Quatre Mares works, following overhaul. Y9072 was rebuilt from Y7427.

VFLI BB424, 8 February 2014

BB424 is seen stabled at Rogerville stabling point, north-west France. This loco is operated by VFLI, Voies Ferrées Locales et Industrielles, which is a subsidiary of SNCF. BB424 was renumbered from BB 63741, and is seen branded up with Normandie Rail Services logos.